AF228174

EXPLORING NATURE

Spotting Amphibians

BY SAMANTHA S. BELL

Kids Core
An Imprint of Abdo Publishing
abdobooks.com

CONTENTS

Only a small percentage
of tadpoles survive
to adulthood.

CHAPTER 1

Rainy Day Surprise

Sam looked out the window. It had been raining for almost a week. He was glad to see that the sun had finally come out.

"Come on, Ella!" he called to his sister. "Let's see how many puddles we can find!"

Sam and Ella slipped on their rain boots. Sam noticed that the small ditch near the front yard was full of water.

"Look, Ella," Sam said. "There's something swimming in the water!"

Ella reached down and carefully scooped up some of the water in her hands. Tiny creatures wriggled around. "Are these fish?" Ella asked.

"Those are tadpoles," Sam said. "They are baby frogs. They hatch from eggs in the water. As they get bigger, they will grow legs. Soon they'll be able to hop on land."

Ella watched the tadpoles swim. She wanted to come back here every day. She couldn't wait to watch them change!

It is important to be gentle when handling amphibians.

Salamander larvae look more similar to their adult forms than tadpoles do.

A Special Kind of Animal

Amphibians are a group of animals that includes frogs, toads, newts, salamanders, and caecilians (pronounced sih-SIHL-yuhns).

Scientifically, toads are a type of frog. But most people use *frog* and *toad* to refer to animals with certain physical and behavioral differences. The word *amphibian* comes from a Greek word that means "double life." Almost all amphibians spend part of their lives in water and part on land.

Beneath the Surface

Caecilians are amphibians that look like large worms or shiny snakes. They have no legs. Most live deep underground. They do not need to see or hear. Because of this, their eyes are very small or hidden under the skin. They have no ear holes. They are not native to the United States. But some were found in Florida in 2021.

abdobooks.com

Published by Abdo Publishing, a division of ABDO, PO Box 398166, Minneapolis, Minnesota 55439. Copyright © 2026 by Abdo Consulting Group, Inc. International copyrights reserved in all countries. No part of this book may be reproduced in any form without written permission from the publisher. Kids Core™ is a trademark and logo of Abdo Publishing.

Printed in the United States of America, North Mankato, Minnesota.
102025
012026

THIS BOOK CONTAINS
RECYCLED MATERIALS

Cover Photo: Steve Bower/Shutterstock Images
Interior Photos: Shutterstock Images, 4–5, 8, 12–13, 18, 28 (top right), 28 (bottom left), 28 (bottom right), 29; Zivica Kerkez/Shutterstock Images, 7; Ken Griffiths/Shutterstock Images, 10; FatCamera/E+/Getty Images, 15; Joe McDonald/Shutterstock Images, 16; Jacob Loyacano/Shutterstock Images, 20–21; Mike Redmer/Shutterstock Images, 22 (top); iStockphoto, 22 (bottom); Nathan A. Shepard/Shutterstock Images, 25; ER Degginger/Science Source, 26; Irina Gutyryak/Shutterstock Images, 28 (top left)

Editor: Marie Pearson
Series Designer: Marley Richmond

Library of Congress Control Number: 2025939178

Publisher's Cataloging-in-Publication Data

Names: Bell, Samantha S., author.
Title: Spotting amphibians / by Samantha S. Bell
Description: Minneapolis, Minnesota: Abdo Publishing, 2026 | Series: Exploring nature | Includes online resources and index.
Identifiers: ISBN 9781098298692 (lib. bdg.) | ISBN 9798384932499 (ebook)
Subjects: LCSH: Amphibians--Juvenile literature. | Amphibians--Behavior--Juvenile literature. | Zoology--Juvenile literature. | Nature--Juvenile literature. | Ecological science--Juvenile literature. | Habitats (Ecology)--Juvenile literature.
Classification: DDC 597.80--dc23

Amphibians cannot create their own body heat. Instead, they must rely on the environment to warm up or cool down. They use shade, sunlight, and more to do this.

Tiny Creatures, Big Jobs

Amphibians play an important role in their ecosystems. They are both predators and prey.

They eat insect pests. They are a food source for larger animals.

There are more than 8,700 species of amphibians around the world. They can be found on all continents except Antarctica. They live in forests, deserts, rivers, and mountains. With so many kinds in so many places, it's fun to search for amphibians!

Explore Online

Look at the website below. Does it give any new information about amphibians that wasn't in Chapter One?

What Are Amphibians?

abdocorelibrary.com/spotting -amphibians

People should not put their hands into places they cannot see when catching amphibians. Tools such as a net can help.

CHAPTER 2

Looking for Amphibians

Amphibians may be hard to find at first. Many hide under rocks, leaf piles, and logs. In the summer, they need shelter from the heat. In the winter, they need protection from the cold. Staying under cover also helps keep them safe from predators.

People do not need a lot of equipment to find amphibians. When looking for amphibians in water, they may use a small net. The net can help them catch the animal so they can observe it more easily. A magnifying glass can help them get a closer look. They may take a photo of the animal. Then they can gently let it go in the same place where it was caught.

Toads and frogs hatch from eggs in the spring. The babies are called tadpoles. People can find tadpoles in **standing water**, ponds, and slow-moving streams. Over time, a tadpole grows legs, and its tail disappears. Then it can go on land.

Toads spend more time on dry land. People can find them in yards, parks, **wetlands**,

A magnifying glass can give a close look at amphibians without touching them.

or forests. Depending on the **climate**, toads can be active from April to November. They usually hide during the day when it is warm. They come out at night when the weather cools off.

People rarely see spring peeper frogs, but their calls can often be heard in the spring.

People can find frogs around ponds, damp gardens, lakes, and swamps. This is because frogs drink and breathe through their skin. They must stay clean and moist. Like toads, frogs are mostly active at night. Some species can be heard chirping at dawn and dusk.

Searching for Salamanders

Salamanders also need to be moist to survive. Most prefer a cool, damp **habitat**. This helps many of them breathe through their skin. A good time to find salamanders is in the spring or fall when the weather is cooler. Salamanders are also more active after it rains.

Spotting Eggs

Most amphibians lay eggs. These are called spawn. Frog and toad spawn are easy to spot. Frog spawn looks like big clumps of jelly. Toads lay long strings of eggs. These are usually wrapped around plants in the water.

Hiding under rocks can help keep a salamander's skin from drying out quickly in the sunlight.

Some salamanders are found in streams and ponds. On land, people can look under bark, logs, and rocks. When searching for salamanders, it is important to put these objects back again. That way, the salamanders are not disturbed.

Hellbenders are huge salamanders in North America. Scientist Andy Hill wants to help the **endangered** eastern hellbender. He said:

> Hellbenders are difficult to find. . . . We identify quality habitat and look for clear, cold-running water. We look under every rock and [crack]. You train your eye to look for movement—a blinking eye, a flash.

Source: Graeme Green. "Meet the Snot Otter." *BBC*, 8 Sept. 2024, bbc.com. Accessed 14 May 2025.

Comparing Texts

Does this quote support the information in this chapter? Or does it give a different perspective? Write a few sentences to explain your answer.

Getting an up-close look can help when identifying an amphibian.

Identifying Amphibians

At first glance, toads and frogs look similar. But they do have some differences. Toads have shorter hind legs. Their legs are better for short hops and walking. Frogs have long, powerful back legs for leaping. Their back feet are often webbed for swimming.

Frog or Toad?

There are several ways to tell a toad from a frog.

Toads and frogs have different types of skin too. Toads have dry, thick skin. This helps them hold in moisture. The skin is rough and bumpy. It helps them blend into their surroundings. Frogs have thin skin. It can take in water and oxygen. Frogs are usually smooth and slimy.

There are many species of toads and frogs. People look at different traits to identify them. They look at the color and the patterns on the skin. They listen for the sounds the animals make. Each species of toad and frog has its own call. The habitat can also provide clues.

Spotting Salamanders

Salamanders have tails as adults. They usually have long bodies and short legs.

Their legs are so short that their stomachs touch the ground. All salamanders need to keep their skin moist. But they do not all have smooth skin. Newts are a type of salamander. They usually have rough, warty skin that looks dry.

Salamanders come in many colors and patterns. Looking at these is a good way to identify salamanders. These amphibians can

Life Underwater

Some salamanders never leave the water. Axolotls are salamanders that never grow out of their water stage. They keep their gills and stay underwater. Sirens are also salamanders that stay underwater. They have two front legs but no back legs.

After a larval stage, eastern newts enter an eft stage, *pictured*. In this stage, they develop lungs and live on land until they reach adulthood. Then they return to living in the water.

be brown, black, gray, green, yellow, red, or orange. Some are spotted or striped.

Size is another way to identify salamanders. Most species are under 6 inches (15 cm) long.

Mudpuppies can be 8 to 19 inches (20–49 cm) long.

But some are very large. Hellbenders can grow up to 29 inches (74 cm) long.

Paying attention to what an amphibian looks like is a good way to tell what it is.

A field guide is a book with pictures and facts. It can help people identify exactly what kinds of amphibians they find. Looking for amphibians helps people learn about the world around them!

Further Evidence

Look at the article below. Does it give any new evidence to support Chapter Three?

Frogs, Salamanders, and Caecilians

abdocorelibrary.com/spotting
-amphibians

Field Notes

Magnifying glass

Rain boots

Net

Camera

Amphibian Log

Species name:
Northern leopard frog

Date:
June 8

Time of day:
Evening

Weather:
Cloudy

Location:
Near pond at park

Habitat where found:
In the grass uphill from the pond

Sketch:

Physical features:
Smooth skin; greenish brown with dark spots; two lines running down each side

A blank Amphibian Log is available at **abdocorelibrary.com**.

Glossary

climate

the average weather in an area over a long period of time

ecosystems

communities of living and nonliving things that interact with each other

endangered

at risk of dying out

habitat

the natural environment where a plant or animal lives

standing water

water that does not move or flow, such as puddles

wetlands

low areas of land covered with shallow water, such as swamps or marshes

Online Resources

To learn more about spotting amphibians, visit our free resource websites below.

Visit **abdocorelibrary.com** or scan this QR code for free Common Core resources for teachers and students, including vetted activities, multimedia, and booklinks, for deeper subject comprehension.

Visit **abdobooklinks.com** or scan this QR code for free additional online weblinks for further learning. These links are routinely monitored and updated to provide the most current information available.

Learn More

Andrews, Elizabeth. *How Amphibians Evolved.* Abdo, 2024.

Lombardo, Jennifer. *The World of Frogs.* Cavendish Square, 2025.

Index

About the Author

Samantha S. Bell lives in the foothills of the Blue Ridge Mountains with her family and four cats. She has written more than 150 nonfiction books for students from kindergarten through high school. Some of her favorite amphibians to spot are young eastern newts, also called red efts.